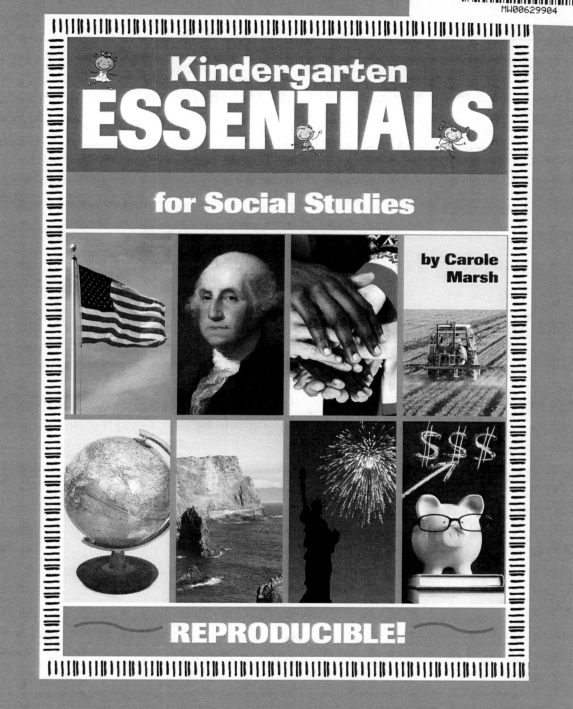

Kindergarten ESSENTIALS

for Social Studies

by Carole Marsh

REPRODUCIBLE!

Dear Teachers,

Have you ever wished you had everything you needed to teach social studies in one easy-to-use resource? Now you have it in *Kindergarten Essentials for Social Studies.* Even in kindergarten, students are expected to learn a lot! This book will help you meet essential state standards with age-appropriate activities in a fun, attractive, and interesting style!

In addition to almost 100 reproducible activity pages, this book offers even more hands-on learning opportunities with templates, graphic organizers, writing prompts, project-based learning ideas, and vocabulary cards with definitions. The writing prompts and vocabulary cards are designed so you can cut them out individually. You can mix and match these "extras" to topics you are studying, to activity pages in the book, or use them on their own.

What is my goal with this book? I want to make your life easier as you introduce your students to the social studies topics and skills they absolutely need to know. I am confident this book accomplishes exactly that!

From my desk to yours,

Your Kindergarten Essentials are already attractive and fun (in addition to educational, of course), but you can customize them to make them colorful and unique!

Copy Writing Prompts and Vocabulary Cards onto colored paper. Choose colors that match your classroom decorative theme, a theme for social studies materials, or use an assortment of colors. Or, as an alternative, copy them onto white paper, and use your markers, highlighters, stickers, and glitter-glue to add personalization and pizzazz to the borders. Either way, laminate them so they last!

P.S. I would LOVE to see what you come up with! Connect with me at Gallopade on Facebook or Pinterest.

Table of Contents

History & Civics

Economics

Appendix

What Comes First?

First means happening before anything else.

#1

Pam   Bob   Jan   Ron

Homeroom

Answer the questions.

1. Who will be first to homeroom? _____

2. When do you like to be first? _____

_____

WHAT COMES NEXT?

Next means happening <u>right after</u> something else.

Jan   Bob   Pam   Ron

MATH

Ron will write on the chalkboard first.

Then, _____ will write on the chalkboard next.

///

It is time to brush your teeth.
Write F under what you do first.
Write N under what you do next.

_____   _____

LAST BUT NOT LEAST

Last means happening after everything else.

Answer the questions.

1. Who will get on the bus first? _____

2. Who will get on the bus next? _____

3. Who will get on the bus last? _____

Have you ridden on a school bus? ☐ Yes ☐ No

TOOLS TO MEASURE TIME

People use <u>tools</u> to keep track of time and events.

We use a **clock** to know what time it is.
A clock can tell us when it is time to wake up.

We use a **calendar** to know what day it is.
A calendar can remind us of special days like holidays.

We use a **timeline** to learn about events in history.
A timeline shows events in the order they occurred.

Match each tool to how we can use it.

to get to school on time

to remember your aunt's birthday

to learn about events in U.S. history

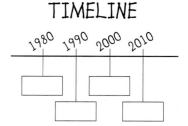

TIMELINE

1980   1990   2000   2010

TODAY

Today is now.
Something happening now is happening today.

Put a ⭐ in the box that marks today.

Calendar

Sunday	Monday	Tuesday	Wednesday	Thursday	Friday	Saturday

What day is it today? _____

Check the things you will do today.

Yesterday

Something happening now is happening today.
The day before today was **yesterday**.
Yesterday has already happened.

Put a ⭐ **in the box that marks today.**

Write "Y" on the day that was yesterday.

Calendar

Sunday	Monday	Tuesday	Wednesday	Thursday	Friday	Saturday

What day is it today? _____

What day came before today? _____

What day was yesterday? _____

What did you do yesterday? _____

_____

Tomorrow

Today is happening now.
Yesterday already happened.
The day after today is tomorrow.
Tomorrow has not happened yet!

Put a ⭐ in the box that marks today.

Write "T" on the day that is tomorrow.

Calendar

Sunday	Monday	Tuesday	Wednesday	Thursday	Friday	Saturday

What day is today? _____

What comes after today? _____

What day is tomorrow? _____

What will you do tomorrow? _____

_____

Days and Weeks

There are seven days in a week.

They are Sunday, Monday, Tuesday, Wednesday, Thursday, Friday, and Saturday.

1. Say the days of the week out loud.

2. Circle Monday in yellow.

3. Circle the day after Monday in green.

4. Circle Friday in red.

5. Circle the day before Friday in blue.

Calendar

Sunday	Monday	Tuesday	Wednesday	Thursday	Friday	Saturday
1	2	3	4	5	6	7

WHAT MONTH IS IT?

This calendar shows one **month**. Most months have four weeks, with a few days left over.

Calendar

Sunday	Monday	Tuesday	Wednesday	Thursday	Friday	Saturday
1	2	3	4	5	6	7
8	9	10	11	12	13	14
15	16	17	18	19	20	21
22	23	24	25	26	27	28
29	30	31				

Color each week of the calendar a different color.

Then answer the questions.

1. How many days are in each week?_____

2. How many days are in this month?_____

3. How many complete weeks are in this month? _____

4. How many days are left over in this month? _____

Have a Great Year!

There are 12 months in a **year**. They are:

1. January 2. February 3. March

4. April 5. May 6. June

7. July 8. August 9. September

10. October 11. November 12. December

Answer the questions.

1. How many months are in a year? _____

2. What month is first?

_____

3. What month is last?

_____

4. What month is after October?

_____

5. What month is before May?

_____

PAST, PRESENT, FUTURE

The **past** is time that already happened.

The **present** is today.

The **future** is tomorrow and the time to come after that.

Nan is 12 years old.
This is a timeline of Nan's life.
Timelines show events in the order they happen.

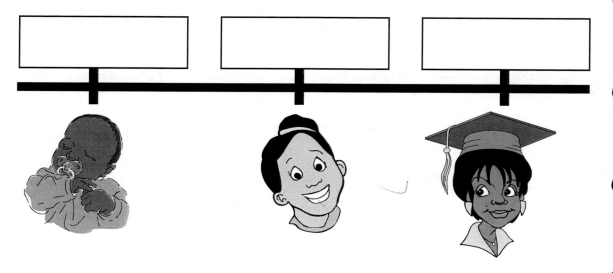

Write "past" above the picture from Nan's <u>past</u>.

Write "present" above the picture in Nan's <u>present</u>.

Write "future" above the picture that shows Nan's <u>future</u>.

Long Ago

Something that happened long ago is called history.

Things that happened long ago happened in the past.

Circle the picture that shows something from long ago.

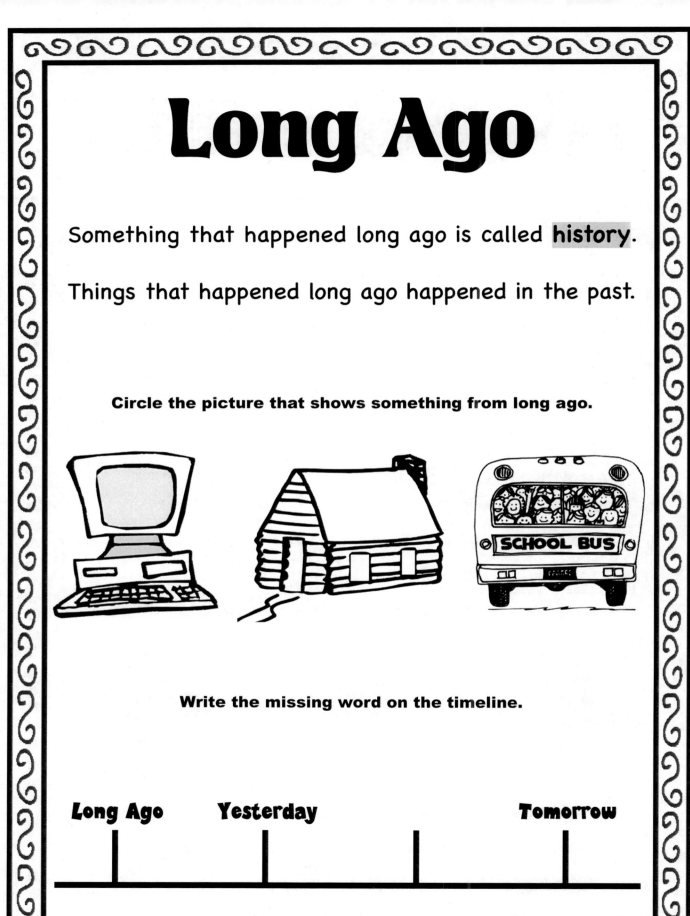

Write the missing word on the timeline.

| Long Ago | Yesterday | | Tomorrow |

MY LiFE

You have a history.

Things that happened in your life are part of your history.

You can tell about your history with pictures and stories.

Write 1 next to the <u>first</u> event in your life.

Write 2 next to the <u>second</u> event in your life.

Write 3 next to the <u>third</u> event in your life.

☐ I was born.   ☐ I started kindergarten.   ☐ I learned to walk.

Terrific Timelines

Timelines show events in the order they occurred. This order is called <u>chronological order.</u>

A timeline is a useful tool to show changes over time.

This timeline shows changes in housing over time:

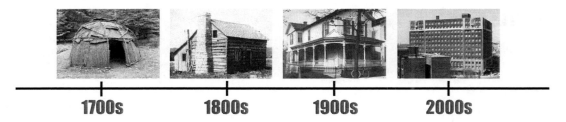

1700s   1800s   1900s   2000s

Draw 3 events in your life to show change over time.

(Put them in <u>chronological order</u> from left to right.)

Add a description or year under each box.

My Personal Timeline

Learn About the Past

We can learn about the past from stories.

People in our community can share their stories with us. Their stories help us learn how our community has changed over time!

Ask a parent or grandparent to tell you a story about an event in their life. Next, draw a picture of the event.
Then, share the story with your class.

Primary Sources

A **primary source** is a record of an event made by a person who was there when the event occurred.

Examples of primary sources:

photographs   letters   diaries   **+ stories about events told by people who were there**

We can use primary sources to learn about the past.
We can compare what we learn about the past to our daily lives today!

Use the photograph to compare life in the past to the present.

Children working at a factory in 1909

Is this photograph a primary source? ___ yes   ___ no

What can you learn about the past from the photo?

_____

How was life in the past different from life today?

_____

Artifact Detective

Artifacts are <u>objects</u> people used in the past.
An artifact is also a <u>primary source</u>.

Examples of artifacts:

tools   weapons   dishes

Artifacts help us learn how people lived in the <u>past</u>.

Things we use today could become artifacts studied in the future!

Complete the table:
Write P by the artifacts from the past.
Write T by the items people use today.

Items Used in Daily Life

to get food	🛒		⬥	
to write messages	⌨		🖥	
to travel	🚗		🐎	
to listen to music	📻		🎧	

Up and Down

If you throw something in the air, it goes **up**.
When it falls back to the ground, it comes **down**.

Color the picture of a boy flying a kite.

Answer the questions.

1. Which object is up? _____

2. Which object is down? _____

HERE AND THERE

Things that are near us are here.
Things that are farther away from us are there.
Here and there are words that show distance.

Write H by the animal nearest the boy.

Write T by the animal farther away from the boy.

Color the picture.

Front and Back

Everything has a **front** and **back**. This book has a front and back. Even you have a front and back!

Color the pictures that show the front red.
Color the pictures that show the back blue.

NEAR AND FAR

Something **near** is close to you.
Something **far** is distant from you.

Near and far describe location.

Write N by the animal near the boy.
Write F by the animal far from the boy.
Color the pictures.

Above and Below

Something **above** you is <u>over</u> you.
Something **below** you is <u>under</u> you.

Above and below describe <u>location</u>.

Draw a square around something above the boy.
Draw a circle around something below the boy.
Color the picture.

LEFT AND RIGHT

Left and right describe location.

 Left is this direction.

Right is this direction.

Which side of the room is the door on?
☐ left ☐ right

Which side of the room is the window on?
☐ left ☐ right

Color the picture.

door   window

In Front Of & Behind

Something **in front of** you is <u>ahead</u> of you.
Something **behind** you is in <u>back</u> of you or
<u>after</u> you.

In front of and behind describe <u>location</u>.

Write F under the person in the <u>front</u> of the line.
Write B under all the people <u>behind</u> the first person.

_____ _____ _____ _____

Do you like to be in front or behind at lunch time?

_____

Before and After

Before means <u>sooner than</u> something else. It can also mean <u>in front of</u> someone or something else.

After means <u>later than</u> something else. It can also mean <u>behind</u> someone or something else.

Answer the questions.

1. Will Ron get to lunch before or after Bob?

_____

2. Will Pam get to lunch before or after Jan?

_____

3. How many people will get to lunch before Bob?

_____

Geography Fun!

Geography is the study of places on Earth. Geography includes where places are located. Geography also includes what places are like.

Geography helps us learn about our community.
Circle the pictures of things in your community.

mountain

ocean

lighthouse

church

park

lake

river

houses

playground

signal

hill

trees

Geography **words** and **tools** help us <u>describe</u> and <u>find</u> where places are located. They also help us learn what places are like.

Cardinal Directions

Cardinal directions are the directions <u>north</u>, <u>south</u>, <u>east</u>, and <u>west</u>.

A **compass rose** is a symbol that shows cardinal directions on a map.

Label the compass rose with cardinal directions:

- **Write N for north in the box on the top of the compass rose.**
- **Write S for south in the box on the bottom of the compass rose.**
- **Write E for east in the box on the right of the compass rose.**
- **Write W for west in the box on the left of the compass rose.**

N

W   E

S

WHERE DO YOU LIVE?

Your home address identifies where you live.
Your address helps friends find your house to visit.
Your address helps mail carriers find your
house to deliver mail.

Your home address:

Your name:	
Your house or apartment number and street name:	
Your city:	
Your state:	
Your ZIP code:	
Your country:	

SPECIAL PROJECT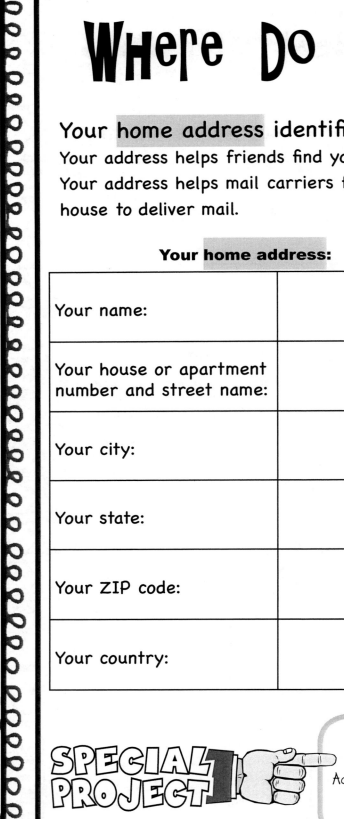

Write a letter to yourself.
You could write about your day.
Address an envelope with your home address.
Put the letter in the envelope.
Put a stamp on the envelope and mail it!

Getting Around Your Town!

You have a home address. All of the other homes and businesses in your town have addresses, too.

When you know an address, you can find your way around your town!

Use the map to answer the questions.

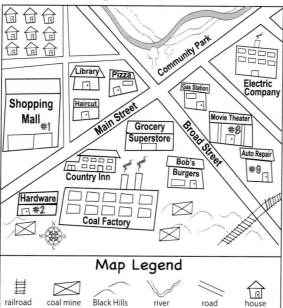

What is at 2 Main Street?

_____

What is at 8 Broad Street?

_____

How many houses are behind the shopping mall?

_____

What street is in front of Country Inn?

_____

MAP FUN!

A **map** is a drawing of Earth.

Maps show what places look like from <u>above</u>.
Maps show places <u>smaller</u> than they really are.

Maps are useful tools!
Maps help us find where things are located.

In each pair, circle the picture that shows a view from above.

Side view

**Here is
an example.**

View from above

1

2

MAPS

Maps represent real places on Earth.

This is a map of North America.

You live on the continent of North America.

Map of North America

USA

Canada

USA

Mexico

Color each country on the map a different color.

GLOBES

A **globe** is a round <u>model</u> of Earth.

Globes show what places look like from <u>above</u>.
Globes show places <u>smaller</u> than they really are.

Globes are useful tools!
Globes help us find where things are located.

Circle the pictures that show globes.

Do globes show Earth larger or smaller than Earth?

❑ larger   ❑ smaller

model: a simple item that shows key features of a real item; models are usually smaller than the real objects they stand for

LAND AND WATER

Maps and globes show **land features**.
Maps and globes show **water features**.
They show land and water in <u>different colors</u>.

Water is usually <u>blue</u> on maps and globes.
Land is usually <u>green</u> on maps and globes.

Color the <u>land</u> green on the map and globe.
Color the <u>water</u> blue on the map and globe.

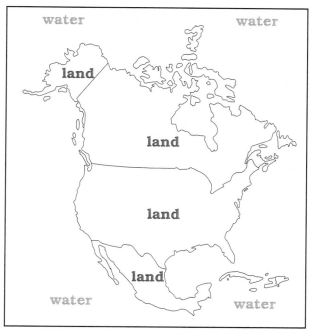

Map Legend

Maps use **symbols** to show where things are located. A **map legend** explains what each symbol means. A map legend can also be called a **map key**.

Map symbols help you answer these questions:

Where is something located?   What is a place like?

What is near a place?   What is far from a place?

Circle the map legend in blue.

Trace the roads on the map in red.

Circle where the school is located in green.

What is the airport near? _____

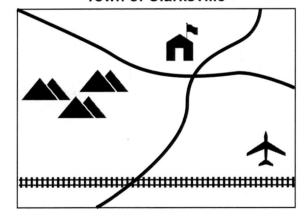

Town of Clarksville

Map Legend

Road
Railroad
Mountains
Airport
School

symbol: a picture or thing that stands for something else

Maps Vary

Different maps show different things.

For example: Some maps show water and mountains.

Some maps show roads and cities and houses.

 You can use maps to find where people and things are located in your community.

Create a map of your classroom.
Use symbols to show where the door, desks, and other items are located.
Add a map legend to explain what each symbol means.

Map Legend

Geographic Features

Geography includes the study of location, climate, and physical surroundings.

Location

where a place is; where people live

Climate

the kind of weather an area has over a long period of time

Physical Surroundings

landforms and bodies of water in an area

Picture 1

Picture 2

1. Circle words that describe the geography shown in the first picture in blue.

2. Circle words that describe the geography shown in the second picture in red.

mountains   dry   snowy

hot   desert

Geography Affects How We Live

Geography affects how people meet their basic wants such as <u>food</u>, <u>clothing</u>, and <u>housing</u>.

People in cold climates need clothes and houses to keep them warm.
People in hot climates need clothes and houses to keep them cool.

Write C under the items people use in a <u>cold</u> climate.
Write H under the items people use in a <u>warm</u> climate.

_____   _____   _____

Today, most people buy food at the grocery store.
In the past, most people got food from their surroundings.

Match each person from the past with their food.

I live in a forest.

I live near the ocean.

I live near a river.

Geography Affects Travel & Fun

Geography affects how people travel.
Geography also affects what people do for fun.

Write M by people enjoying geography of a <u>mountain</u> town.
Write B by people enjoying geography of a <u>beach</u> town.

What do you like to do outside for fun?

_____

Four Seasons

A **season** is one of the four phases of the year. The four seasons are <u>spring</u>, <u>summer</u>, <u>fall</u>, and <u>winter</u>.

As seasons change throughout the year, the weather in your community changes too.

Color the pictures of the four seasons.

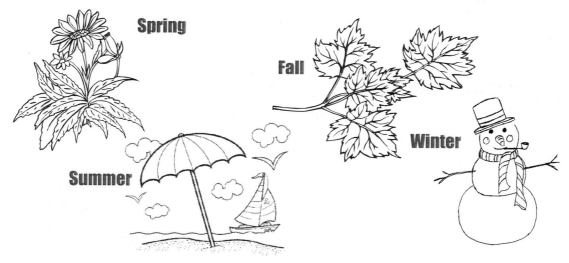

Spring

Fall

Summer

Winter

Match each item to the season when it is used.

Winter   Summer

Families Change

Families **change** over time.

In the past, families made their own clothes and grew their own food. They did not have television or phones. Everyone worked hard to survive!

Today, families buy food and clothes in stores. They drive cars, talk on cellphones, and watch movies. Inventions make many family chores easier than in the past!

Write P by the items used by a family in the past.
Write T by the items used by a family today.

COMMUNITIES CHANGE

Communities **change** over time.

In the <u>past</u>, communities were smaller. They had fewer people and fewer businesses. Communities did not provide many services.

<u>Today</u>, communities are larger. Some communities have huge populations. Some have tall buildings. Communities today provide many services like police and traffic lights and clean water.

Write P under the map that shows a community in the <u>past</u>.
Write T under the map that shows a community <u>today</u>.

Miller Town in 1915

Miller Town today

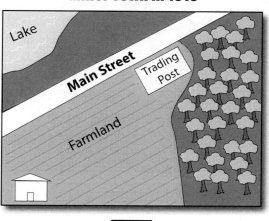

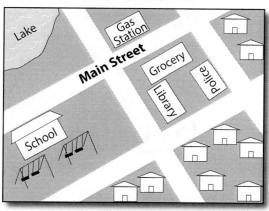

Describe how Miller Town changed over time:

_____

_____

SCHOOLS CHANGE

Schools **change** over time.

In the <u>past</u>, many schools only had one room and one teacher. Students of all ages had class together. Children had to walk a long way to school. Students wrote on slate with chalk.

<u>Today</u>, schools have different classes for different ages. Children who live far away can ride a bus. Today, students have books, paper, and computers. Most students go to school much longer today too!

Look at the photographs.
Then choose the best answer to each question.

School in the past

School today

Is the photograph of the school in the past a primary source?
____ yes   ____ no

Is the photograph of the school today a primary source?
____ yes   ____ no

What can you learn from these photographs?
____ Schools today are the same as schools in the past.
____ Schools today are a lot different from schools in the past.

Transportation Changes

Transportation **changes** over time.

 WORDS TO KNOW!

> **transportation:** a way of moving people and things from one place to another

In the <u>past</u>, transportation was by horse, wagon, ship, or on foot. <u>Next</u>, trains and steamboats became a faster way to travel. <u>Today</u> people travel in cars and airplanes. Ships and trains quickly move food and goods. Subways and buses provide rides too.

Imagine the future...

Self-driving cars?   Solar cars?   Quick trips to Mars?

Draw an example of transportation from the past.

Past

Draw what transportation might look like in the future.

Future

COMMUNITY

A **community** is where people live, work, and play.

You live in a community.
You play in a community.
You go to school in a community.

This family is enjoying a picnic at their community park. But it is no ordinary day!

Circle all the wacky things in the picture!

You can be a **good citizen** in your community.

Be Kind

Good citizens are kind.
Kindness is gentle and caring behavior.

You are kind when you are <u>nice</u> to other people.
You are kind when you try to make people feel <u>better</u>.

Write "kind" under the pictures that show kindness.
Write X under the pictures that do <u>not</u> show kindness.

_____   _____

_____   _____

Take Turns and Share

Good citizens **take turns**. Good citizens **share**. Taking turns and sharing lets everyone participate.

When you take turns at recess, you give other people a chance to play.

When you share crayons in class, you let other people color too.

Circle the pictures of sharing or taking turns.

Read each sentence and put a ✓ if it is true.

☐ I like when people share with me.

☐ I like when people let me have a turn.

BE HONEST

Good citizens are honest.
Honesty is telling the truth.

You are being honest when you tell the truth.
You are NOT being honest when you tell a lie.
You are NOT being honest if you cheat or steal.

Write "honest" under the picture that shows honesty.
Write X under the pictures that do not show honesty.

_____

_____

It is best to be honest, even if it means you don't get what you want.

Self-Control

Good citizens use **self-control**.
Self-control is controlling your own behavior.

Self-control is waiting for your <u>turn</u>.
Self-control is NOT losing your <u>temper</u>.
Self-control is avoiding things that are bad for you.

Circle the pictures that show self-control.
Draw an X over the pictures that do NOT show self-control.

What is a solution when you feel yourself losing self-control?

_____

Take Care of Your Things

Good citizens take care of their things.

Things cost money. Things have value.
Someone worked to provide the things you have.

You show <u>respect</u> and <u>appreciation</u> when
you take care of your things.

Look at each pair of pictures.
Circle the picture that shows how to take care of your things.
Draw an X over the picture that does <u>NOT</u>.

If you do NOT take care of your things, what might happen to them?

_____

Respect Other People's Things

Good citizens <u>respect</u> other people's things.

Do you want someone to break your toys?

No!

So, do not break other people's toys.

Do you want someone to crumple your school work?

No!

So, do not crumple your classmates' papers.

Give respect like you want to receive respect.

Circle the picture that shows how you feel when someone does not respect your belongings.

DO YOUR WORK

Good citizens do their work.

classwork   chores at home   chores at school

When everyone does their work, things work better!

Match each picture to the work it shows.

   **answer math questions**

   **erase the board**

   **organize the bookshelf**

   **throw away the trash**

Work Together

Good citizens work well together. They **cooperate**.

When people work together in groups, they can achieve big goals!

Match each picture to what students are working together to achieve.

start a community garden

build a house of blocks

play a fun game

cook a yummy meal

PARTICIPATION

Good citizens **participate** in <u>making decisions.</u>

You can participate in decisions at home.
You can participate in classroom decisions too.
One day you can participate in community decisions.

Write N by the decisions you can help make <u>now</u>.
Write F by the decisions you can make in the <u>future</u>.

☐ what to watch on tv

☐ what to eat for dinner

☐ what to play at recess

☐ whether to recycle

☐ what charity to help

☐ who to elect as President

 **DISCUSS IT!**

Does your teacher let students help make classroom rules?
What if students decided to have no rules?
Imagine how that would work!

Follow the Rules

Good citizens follow the rules.

Rules help keep people <u>safe</u>.
Rules help keep <u>order</u>.
Rules help make sure everyone is treated <u>fairly</u>.

When people do NOT follow rules, there are consequences.
Consequences for breaking rules are <u>bad results</u>.

**Put an X on the picture that shows
a consequence of NOT following the rule.**

RULE
"Put your toys away."

Rules Everywhere

Home rules help keep order and safety at home.

School rules help keep order and safety at school.

Community rules help keep order and safety in your community.

Read each rule in the table. To complete the "Where" column:
- Write H if it is a rule at <u>home</u>.
- Write S if it is a rule at <u>school</u>.
- Write C if it is a rule in a <u>community</u>.

Read the benefit for following each rule. Under "Consequence" describe what might happen when people break the rule.

Rule	Where	Benefit When Follow Rule	Consequence If Break Rule
Follow the teacher's directions.		The classroom is orderly.	
Put the toys away.		Toys are safe. You can find them.	
Look both ways before crossing the street.		People cross the street safely.	

Making Choices

You make choices every day.

When you make a <u>good</u> choice, you usually get a good result.

When you make a <u>bad</u> choice, you usually get a bad result.

You are responsible for your choices.

You are responsible for your actions.

You are responsible for your results!

Write G by good choices. Write B by bad choices.

Good Citizens

Good citizens help make communities great!

Color these pictures of good citizens.
Circle the things you have done.

Good citizens are trustworthy.

Good citizens take turns.

Good citizens are responsible.

Good citizens are respectful.

Good citizens work together.

Good citizens share.

The truth is...

Good citizens are honest.

With your classmates, make a list of how you can all be good citizens at school. Take turns giving suggestions.

Patriotism

Patriotism is a feeling of love and respect for your country or state.

How can we show our patriotism? Two ways are with:

symbols & holidays

We show respect for **symbols** to honor what they represent.

We celebrate **holidays** to honor and remember people and events important to our community, state, and country.

Our flag is a patriotic symbol.

Color all the flags in this picture.

How many did you find?

_____

A DAY OF THANKSGIVING

Thanksgiving is a holiday to remember when Pilgrims and American Indians shared their food long ago.

We celebrate their cooperation by being thankful for good things in our lives, and with a big feast!

Thanksgiving is celebrated in November.

Color the Thanksgiving feast.

What are you thankful for?

_____

INDEPENDENCE DAY

We celebrate **Independence Day** on July 4th. This is a day to remember when the United States became a country.

We celebrate with parades, fireworks, flags, and cookouts. The Fourth of July is a very patriotic day!

Circle the things we enjoy on Independence Day.

Trace the words to complete the sentence.

Independence Day is also called...

America's birthday

American Flag

The United States **flag** is a symbol of our country.

Our flag has 50 white stars on a blue rectangle.
It has 13 stripes that are red and white.

50 stars for our 50 states today

13 stripes for the 13 colonies
that fought for independence

Color the flag from the past and the flag from today.

1776   **TODAY**

Why did the U.S. flag change over time?

_____

Pledge of Allegiance

The pledge to the American flag is a <u>promise</u> of loyalty to our country. It is called the **Pledge of Allegiance.**

Read and color this page.

"I pledge allegiance

to the Flag of the United States of America

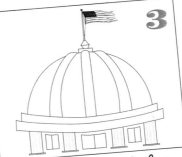

and to the Republic for which it stands:

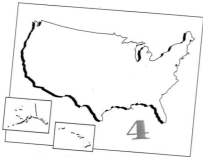

one nation under God, indivisible,

with liberty

and justice

for all."

The word indivisible means "whole, or not divided."

U.S. Leader

The **president** is the <u>leader</u> of the United States.

The president works at the White House in Washington, DC.

Draw the current president at his or her desk.

Write the president's last name here:

_____

- -

_____

Presidents' Day

We honor all presidents of the United States on **Presidents' Day**.

We especially honor **George Washington**.
He was the first president of our country!

Presidents' Day is also called **George Washington Day**.
We celebrate it in February.

**Compare the two pictures of George Washington.
Find 5 differences, and circle them.**

George Washington is called
the "Father of our Country."

Martin Luther King Jr. Day

Dr. Martin Luther King Jr. was an African American. He worked so all people would be treated <u>fairly</u>.

We celebrate **Martin Luther King Jr. Day** in January.

Color the picture of Dr. Martin Luther King Jr.

Trace the word fair.

fair

Draw a picture to show what "fair" means to you.

Happy New Year

New Year's Day is on the first day of the year.
The first day of the year is <u>January 1</u>.

On this holiday, Americans say goodbye to last year.
They wave hello to the new year.

Many people set <u>goals</u> for the new year. *Do you?*

Circle the picture that shows New Year's Day.

Write T for sentences that are <u>true</u>.
Write F for sentences that are <u>false</u>.

_____ 1.   New Year's Day is in February.

_____ 2.   Many people set goals for the new year.

_____ 3.   New Year's Day celebrates good times to come.

MERRY CHRISTMAS

Christmas is a holiday to celebrate the birth of <u>Jesus Christ</u>. Christmas is also a time when people give gifts to their families and friends. At Christmas, Americans like to decorate their homes and enjoy a special meal.

We celebrate Christmas on <u>December 25</u>.

Circle the Christmas traditions.

Columbus Day

Christopher Columbus was an <u>explorer</u>. He sailed for Spain. In 1492, Columbus discovered <u>America</u>!

We celebrate **Columbus Day** in <u>October</u>. We remember Christopher Columbus. We also remember the <u>American Indians</u> who were here first.

Circle the tools that Columbus used on his voyage to America.

VETERANS DAY

On **Veterans Day**, we honor Americans who served in the U.S. <u>armed forces</u>. We celebrate Veterans Day in <u>November</u>. We fly flags and hold parades.

Thank you, veterans!!!

Color these people in the armed forces.

MARINES

AIR FORCE

COAST GUARD

NAVY

ARMY

Memorial Day

On **Memorial Day**, we remember people who fought and <u>died</u> in wars. These veterans made a BIG sacrifice for America. They gave their lives so we could be free.

We celebrate Memorial Day in <u>May</u>.

Circle who we honor on Memorial Day.

Decorate the soldier's grave.

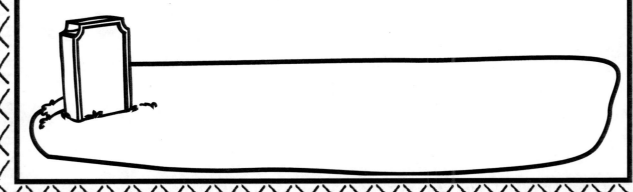

LABOR DAY

Labor Day is a holiday to honor Americans who <u>work</u>.

Labor Day is celebrated in <u>September</u>.
On Labor Day, people relax from work and have picnics and cookouts.

Circle who we honor on Labor Day.

Special Days

All through the year, Americans honor special people and events by celebrating national holidays.

This is a 12-month calendar. It shows a whole year.

January	February	March	April	May	June

July	August	September	October	November	December

Draw a ☮ in January for Martin Luther King Jr. Day.

Draw a ☆ in February for Presidents' Day.

Draw a 🏳 in July for Independence Day.

Draw a 🦃 in November for Thanksgiving.

Draw a ☺ face in the month you were born.

BALD EAGLE

The **bald eagle** is a symbol of the United States. It stands for power, courage, and freedom.

Color the picture of the bald eagle.
Then draw a picture of the eagle's nest.
Don't forget to put eggs in it!

The bald eagle isn't really bald! It has white feathers on its head.

Miss Liberty

The Statue of Liberty is a huge statue in the New York Harbor. It is a symbol of the United States.

It stands for freedom and opportunity.

The copper statue is 151 feet tall from the base to the torch. It stands on a platform that is 154 feet tall.

WORDS TO KNOW!

opportunity: a chance to do something

Color the Statue of Liberty.

Trace each word below.

statue

freedom

opportunity

STAR-SPANGLED BANNER

The **Star-Spangled Banner** is our national anthem. This means it is the official song of the United States.

Sing the Star-Spangled Banner.

O say, can you see, by the dawn's early light,

What so proudly we hailed at the twilight's last gleaming?

Whose broad stripes and bright stars, through the perilous fight,

O'er the ramparts we watched, were so gallantly streaming?

And the rockets' red glare, the bombs bursting in air,

Gave proof through the night that our flag was still there.

O say, does that star-spangled banner yet wave

O'er the land of the free and the home of the brave?

Write the word <u>anthem</u> on the lines.

_____

- -

_____

The Washington Monument

The **Washington Monument** is a symbol of the United States. It was built to honor President <u>George Washington</u>.

We honor George Washington on <u>Presidents' Day</u>.

The Washington Monument is made of marble.

Around the monument are fifty flags. There is one flag for each state.

Complete the dot-to-dot.

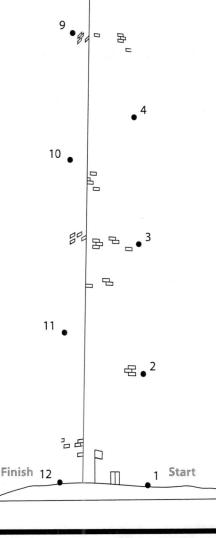

The Washington Monument is 555 feet tall. You can take an elevator to the top to look out!

The Lincoln Memorial

The Lincoln Memorial is a symbol of the United States.

Inside the Lincoln Memorial is a giant statue of President Abraham Lincoln. It is 19 feet tall. It was built to honor President Lincoln.

We honor Abraham Lincoln on Presidents' Day.

Color the Lincoln Memorial.

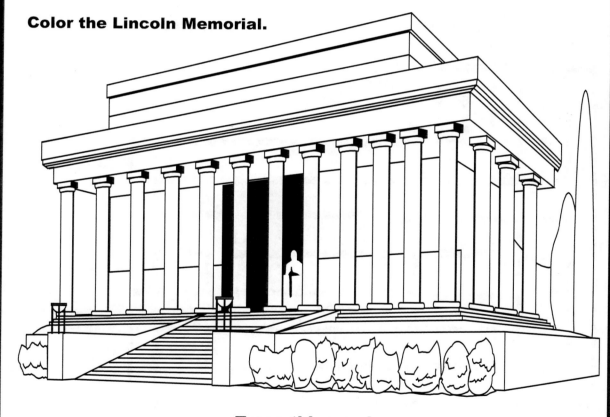

Trace this word.

memorial

THE WHITE HOUSE

The **White House** is a symbol of the United States. The current president of the United States lives in the White House. We honor the president on Presidents' Day.

The White House is a symbol of American <u>democracy</u>.

Help the students find the White House.

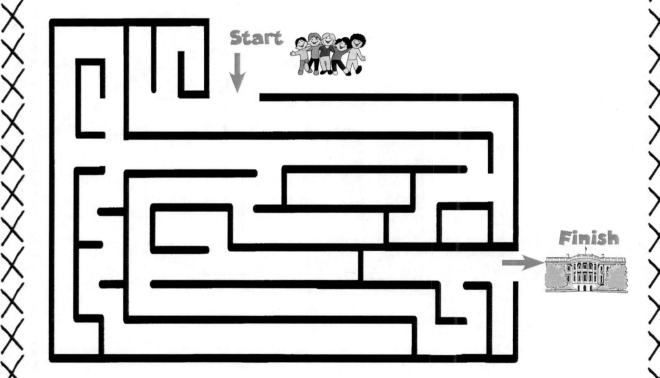

Who lives in the White House?

_____

We Are the Same!
We Are Different!

People are the same in many ways.
We all need food to eat. We all need air to breathe.

People are also unique in many ways.
Some of us have darker skin. Some of us have lighter hair.
Some of us are taller. We may speak different languages.

Draw lines to connect the pictures that are the same.
Circle the ones that are unique.

American Heritage

March

Culture is a way of life. It is your language, food, clothes, celebrations, and customs.

Heritage is ideas and events from the past that help shape today.

Your family's heritage helps shape your culture.

Match each custom with the correct group.

chopsticks

African Americans

Hispanic Americans

piñata

Chinese Americans

American Flag

ALL Americans

Kwanzaa

Customs and Celebrations!

American families and communities have many **customs** and **celebrations**.

Write the number of each celebration by the picture that shows it.

1. Families celebrate birthdays.

2. Many towns celebrate the Fourth of July with parades and fireworks.

3. Chinese Americans celebrate Chinese New Year.

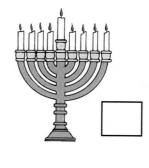

4. Jewish Americans celebrate Hanukkah.

5. Christian Americans celebrate Christmas.

Authority Figures

An **authority figure** is a person who is in charge. Authority figures often make the rules.

At school, the authority figures are the principal and teachers. At home, the authority figures are your parents. Police officers are important authority figures in your community.

Draw lines from authority figures to the pictures of places where you find them.

Mom and Dad   **Teacher**   **Police Officer**

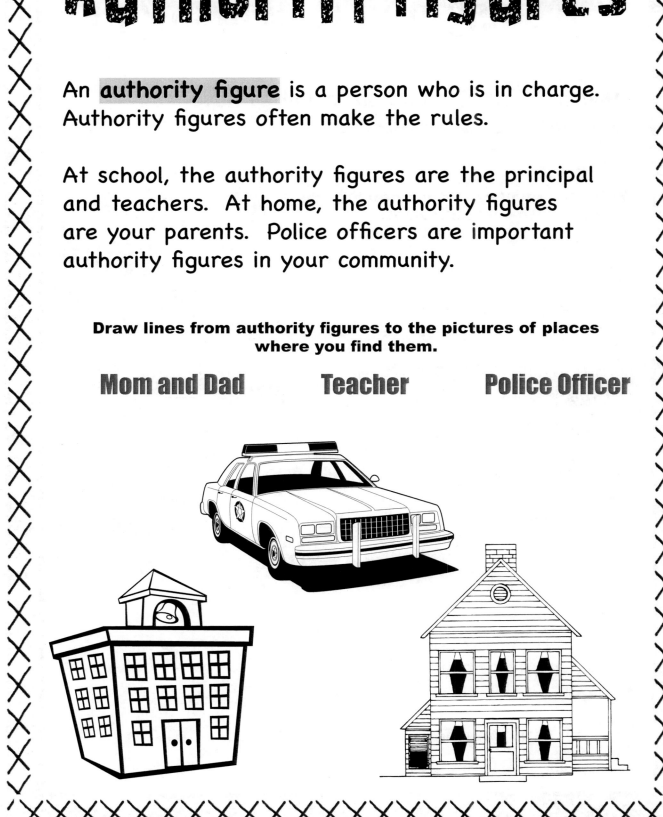

Doctors & Nurses

People do many different **jobs** in your community.

Doctors and **nurses** help people stay healthy.
They also take care of people when they are sick.

Color the pictures of doctors and nurses at work.

What might you like about these jobs?

_____

Construction Workers

Construction workers build houses. They build schools, skyscrapers, and other buildings too!

Circle the tools construction workers use at work.

What might you like about this job?

_____

TEACHERS

Teachers help students learn.
Your teacher helps you learn!

Miss Taylor is getting ready for the first day of school.
Circle the items you think would be useful in her classroom.

What might you like about this job?

_____

CHEFS

Chefs prepare meals for people to eat. Some chefs create their own recipes!

Circle the items that belong in a chef's kitchen.

What might you like about this job?

_____

FARMERS

Farmers grow crops and raise animals.
Most of the food we eat comes from farmers!

WORDS TO KNOW!

crop: a plant grown to be used or sold

Color the pictures in the chart.
Write C by each crop. Write A by each animal.

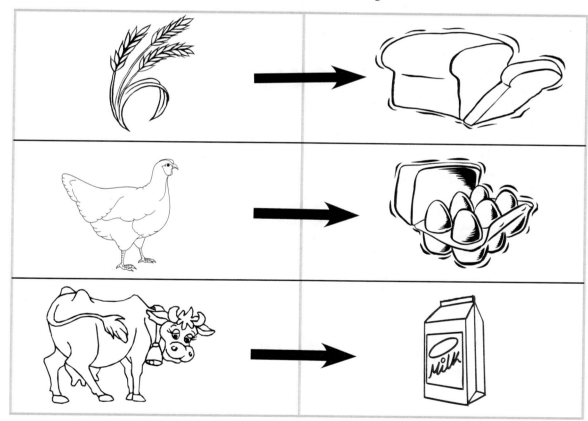

What might you like about this job?

_____

FIREFIGHTERS

Firefighters put out fires.
Firefighters also teach people about fire safety.

Color the picture.
Then circle the house where the firefighter is going.

What might you like about this job?

_____

WORK EARNS MONEY!

People work at **jobs** to earn <u>money</u>.
People use **money** they earn to meet their <u>wants</u>.

People <u>cannot</u> have everything they want.
People must make **choices** about what to buy.

Number the steps in the order they occur.

Joe chooses how to use his money.

Joe buys a new computer game.

Joe cuts grass to earn money.

GOOD CHOICES

People must make choices about what they want.
People choose what to get and what to give up.

How do people make good choices?
Thinking about benefits and costs can help!

A benefit is something good you get. It is an advantage.
A cost is something you give up. It is a disadvantage.

For example:
Sara wants to decide if she should buy a new coloring book.
She wrote down her benefits and costs of buying it.

Benefits:	Costs:
new coloring book	$3.00
I will have lots of fun coloring the pages.	I will not have money to buy candy.

Would you choose to buy the new coloring book?

☐ yes   ☐ no

What items would have big benefits to you?

_____

_____

Needs and Wants

Basic needs are things people must have to live. Food, clothing, and shelter are examples of basic needs.

Wants are things people would like to have.

Write N in the boxes next to the things you <u>need</u>.
Write W in the boxes next to the things you <u>want</u>.

Goods and Services

Goods are things that people make or grow.
We buy goods to satisfy our needs and wants.

Color each good.

//

Services are things people do for other people.
We buy services to satisfy our needs and wants.

Color each service.

WHAT MONEY LOOKS LIKE

Money is also called **currency**.
U.S. currency includes coins and bills.

Coins are money made from metal.
Bills are money made from paper.

Is each form of money a coin or bill?
Circle the right answer.

$1.00 one dollar		coin bill
10¢ dime		coin bill
25¢ quarter		coin bill
1¢ penny		coin bill
$5.00 five dollars		coin bill

MONTH CALENDAR

This month is:

_____

- - - - - - - - - - - - - - - - - -

_____

Sunday	Monday	Tuesday	Wednesday	Thursday	Friday	Saturday

CLOCK

U.S. MAP

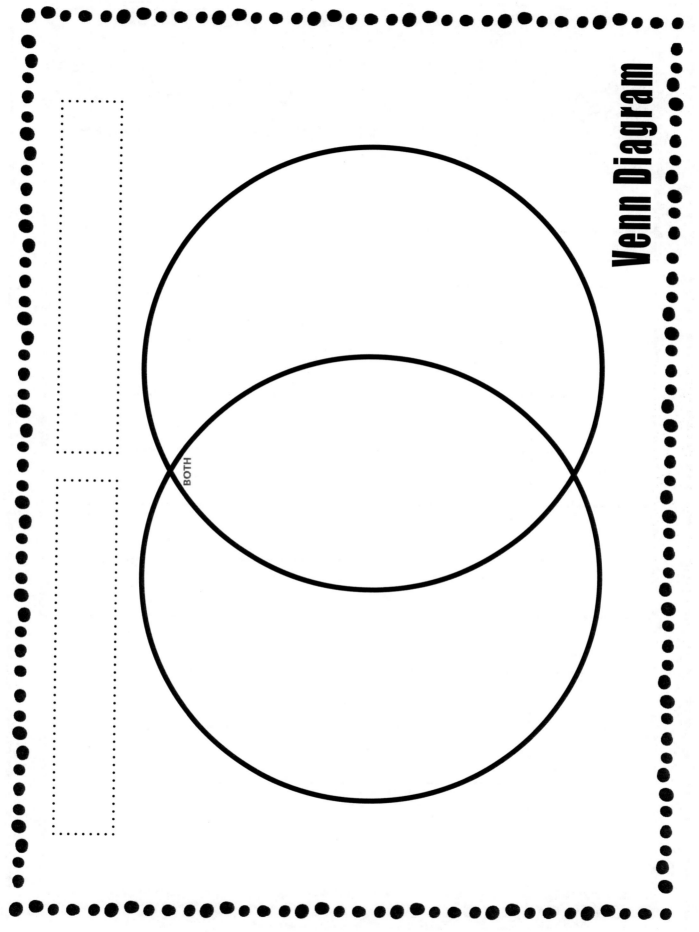

BOTH

Venn Diagram

Acrostic Grid

TOPIC:

Classifying Information

CATEGORY:

CATEGORY:

Five Senses Observation Chart

TOPIC:

Sound

Sight

Touch

Smell

Taste

Five W's

WHERE

WHY

WHO

TOPIC OR EVENT:

WHAT

WHEN

All About Me!

_____

- -

_____

My favorite color

My favorite food

My favorite book

My favorite activity

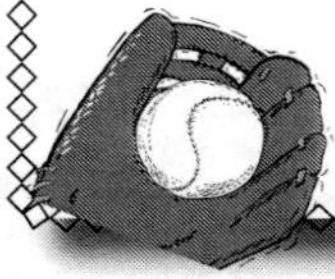

My birthday

This is me!

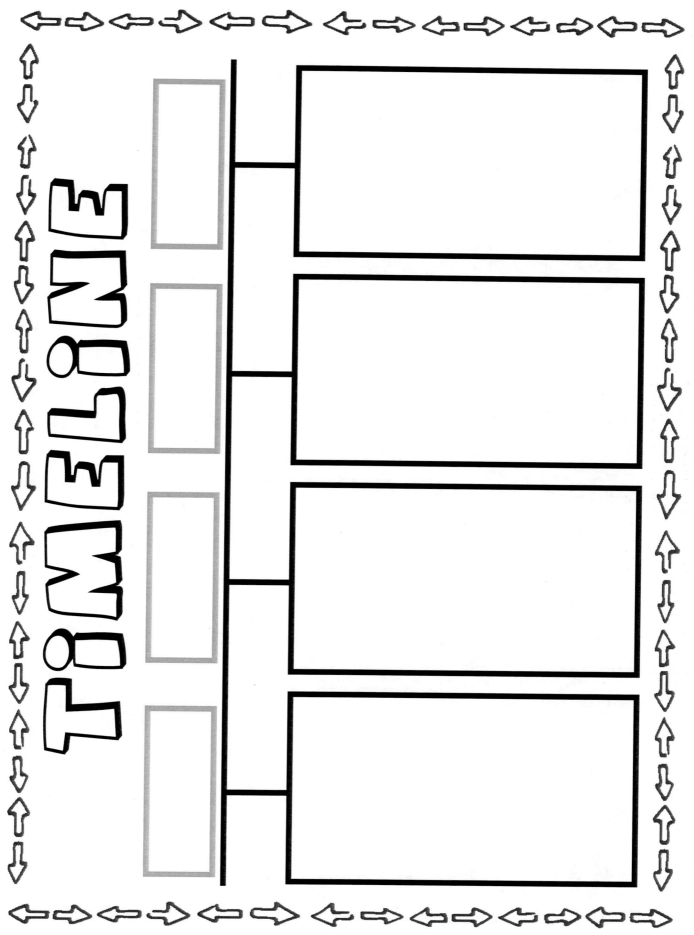

TIMELINE

All About Me Timeline

Year: _____

Year: _____

Year: _____

Year: _____

Birth

Age 1 or 2

Age 3 or 4

Age 5 or 6

_____

_____

_____

_____

_____

_____

_____

_____

_____

_____

_____

_____

My Family Tree

_____

- -

_____

Me

MY STATE FLAG

Write your state's name:

_____

- -

_____

Draw your state flag.

My State Bird

My state bird is the:

_____

- -

_____

_____

- -

_____

Draw your state bird.

MY STATE TREE

My state tree is the:

_____

- -

_____

- -

_____

Draw your state tree.

My State Flower

My state flower is the:

_____

- -

_____

_____

- -

_____

Draw your state flower.

Writing Prompts

MY FAVORITE DAY!

What is your favorite day of the week? Why?

What day comes <u>before</u> your favorite day?

What day comes <u>after</u> your favorite day?

Use a Classroom Calendar

Starting with the beginning of the school year, have students record important upcoming dates like parties and holidays. In addition, have them write down memorable events that happened on a particular day. Show how the calendar can be used to create a classroom history!

WRITE A LETTER

What subject do you like best in school? Write a short letter to your mom or dad to tell them what your favorite subject is, and why. When you finish, write your home address on an envelope and put the letter inside it. Take it home to deliver it!

Writing Prompts

I Know My Holidays!

Choose a holiday that you have learned about.
Write the name of the holiday on a piece of paper.
Draw a picture showing something that represents that holiday.
Then write three words that describe the holiday.

I Have Good Character Traits!

Complete each sentence.

✐ I am courteous when I...
✐ I show loyalty when I...
✐ I show self-control when I...
✐ I am honest when I...
✐ I show respect when I...
✐ I show patience when I...

What I Am Thankful For

Write an acrostic poem using the word "thankful."
For each letter in thankful, think of a word starting with that letter that describes something you are thankful for.
Then decorate your poem with pictures.

Writing Prompts

Climate and Clothing

Think about how climate affects the clothing you wear.

Make a list of clothes that you wear in a cold climate.

Make a list of clothes that you wear in a warm climate.

Draw a picture of each item of clothing next to the words.

Let's Work Together!

What are some ways that you can cooperate with your classmates or work together, in your classroom? Make a list of your ideas on a piece of paper and write why each activity is important.

Share your ideas with your class.

My Favorite State Symbol

Choose a state symbol to write about. Write three sentences about it.

My state symbol is...

I like it because...

My state symbol's colors are...

Writing Prompts

WHAT I WANT TO DO WHEN I GROW UP

Draw a picture of what you want to do when you grow up. Write the name of that job above the picture. Then, write the main thing you will do in that job. For example, if you choose to be a nurse, you might write "help sick people."

FROM FARMERS TO YOU

Make a list of five foods provided by farmers that you like to eat. Write a thank-you letter to a farmer to tell him that you are grateful for the food he or she provides every day. Explain which food is your favorite.

KNOWING THE RULES

Pick a rule in your classroom. Write it on a piece of paper. Write a sentence to explain why the rule is important. Write a second sentence to explain what happens when the rule is not obeyed.

All About Me!

You can use the "All About Me!" template in the book for this activity. At the beginning of the school year, ask students to draw their answers in each block on the page. Have students share their sheets with the class. See how much they have in common!

Additional idea: At the end of the year, have students fill out the "All About Me" template again. This time, see how many blocks they can fill in with words instead of drawings.

What Time Is It?

For this activity, you will need a piece of poster board, paper fasteners, colored card stock and scissors. Draw a large circle on a piece of poster board. Draw the face of a clock onto the circle. With students' help, cut out the clock hands from card stock. Make sure one hand is longer than the other (that will be the minute hand). Use the paper fasteners to attach the hands to the center of the clock.

Ask students to identify things they do at certain times of the day, such as lunch at noon. Write those events on the board. Call out the events one at a time, and select students to come up to the clock and put the clock hands in the correct position for that event.

Variation: Have students make individual clocks using paper plates and move the clock hands appropriately when events are called out. Or, you can use the blank clock template in this book for clock activities.

Create a Brochure Featuring the Four Seasons

Give students a standard piece of paper. Ask them to fold the paper in half, then quarters, so they have four sections. Help them label each section Spring, Summer, Winter, and Fall. Then, ask students to draw something on each section that represents that season. For example, a beach ball could represent summer, or snowflakes could represent winter.

Ask students: What is your favorite season? Why?

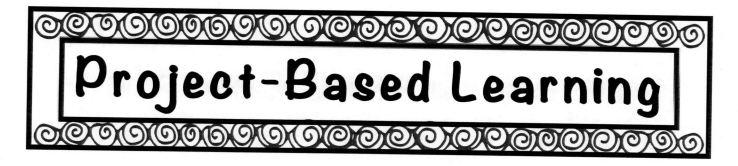

Project-Based Learning

Make a Timeline!

Make a timeline to show your students how time progresses. You can use the timeline template in this book for this activity. You can make a timeline of school activities in a day or a week, a timeline of current events, a timeline of the months of the year…the ideas are endless!

Culture and Family Trees

Read several stories to the class that feature foreign countries and their cultures. Discuss the different cultures represented. Ask students to point out any differences they recognize in the stories regarding food, clothing, art, literature, celebrations, or family structure. Make a list on the board.

Instruct students to ask their parents about their family heritage. Then have each student create a simple family tree using the template in the book. Ask students to present their family trees to the class. How many different cultures are represented? How are they different? How are they the same? Can any of your students speak a second language? Maybe they would be willing to teach the class a few words in that language!

Know Your Directions

Take your students on a tour of the school playground or ballfield. Lead a game of "I Spy" that incorporates directional vocabulary such as "up," "down," "over," "under," "in front of," and "behind." Give the students directional clues about where to find someone or something. For example, you might say, "I spy a girl behind the jungle gym!"

What's the Location?

Read the students a story that mentions a real location. Then help them find that location on a map as well as a globe. What country is it in? In what direction do they have to travel to get to the story's location? Would that be a short trip or a very long trip? How do you know?

Project-Based Learning

Thankfulness Collage

Pass out an index card to each student for this activity. Have each student bring in a picture of something for which they are grateful. They can find pictures in old magazines, bring actual photographs from their home, or print pictures from a computer. Ask each student to write his or her name and what they are thankful for on an index card. Mount the pictures and the index cards on a bulletin board decorated for the Thanksgiving season. As a class, discuss the reasons why students are thankful for their chosen items.

Classroom Holiday

Ask your class to choose a special holiday for their classroom only. Have students follow the steps below, while you write their answers on the board.

1. **What is our special class holiday? Why did we choose it?**

2. **On what day will we celebrate our holiday? Write it on a calendar page and display it in the classroom.**

3. **What things will we do to celebrate our holiday?**

4. **Is there anything special we will wear on our holiday? Draw a picture of it.**

5. **Make invitations to invite other kindergarten classes to your holiday celebration!**

Be a Good Citizen

Lead a class discussion on ways kids can be good citizens. Make a list of students' suggestions, and leave it up for a few days as a reminder. Encourage students to recognize a classmate who shows qualities of good citizenship. Create a certificate or badge for "Citizen of the Week." Make sure students understand exactly why a student won the badge each week.

Chores in the Classroom

What are some chores that need to be done in the classroom? Discuss the question with students and make a list on the whiteboard. Put a checkbox next to each chore. As a student performs each task during the day, have them put a checkmark in the box next to the chore. Ask students why everyone needs to pitch in and help every day. What would happen if they did not?

Project-Based Learning

Working Together in the Community

Send a note home with students. Ask parents to think of an example of people working together in their neighborhood or community to achieve a goal, and have them write a brief explanation of that activity on an index card. Make sure parents also explain the community activity to their child. The next day, gather all the cards. Read each activity aloud, and instruct students to raise their hand when their parents' activity is read aloud. Students will see how much cooperation goes on every day in their communities!

Make a Patriotic Windsock!

Have students make a patriotic windsock to display at their home to show everyone they are a patriot!

Supplies needed include: cylindrical oatmeal box, blue and white construction paper, red and white crepe paper streamers, white yarn or ribbon (strong), and glue, a stapler, scissors, and a hole punch.

Student instructions:

1. **Use scissors to cut off the bottom of the oatmeal box.**

2. **Glue blue construction paper all over the box.**

3. **Draw stars on the white construction paper and cut them out. Glue them on the blue paper covering the box.**

4. **Cut equal sections of red and white crepe paper streamers. Staple them to one end of the oatmeal box.**

5. **Punch four holes, one along each side of the box top. Cut two 12" lengths of yarn or ribbon. Tie the pieces of yarn to opposite sides of the box top.**

6. **Tie a longer piece of yarn to the gathered smaller pieces.**

7. **Hang your patriotic windsock from your window or porch. Show your patriotism!**

Discuss what it means to be patriotic. Why does a patriotic person want to fly the U.S. flag (or the windsock they just made) outside his or her house? What message is that person sending?

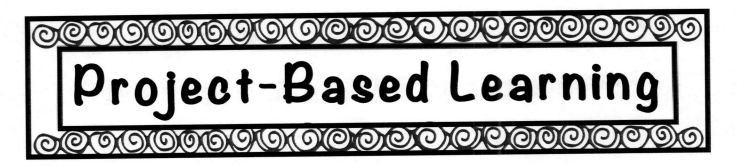

Create Your State Bird

For this activity, students will need modeling clay, index cards, scissors, pipe cleaners, small buttons, a pencil point, glue, and colorful feathers (optional).

Student instructions: Shape a handful of modeling clay into the head and body of the bird. Cut out wings from index cards and stick them into each side of the bird. Glue colorful feathers on the wings and body. Add pipe cleaner legs, button eyes, and a pencil point bill.

Place a staple part way into the top of the bird's body. After the clay dries, slip a string under the staple and hang your bird where the wind will make it sway.

Display idea: Display the bird models along with the "My State Bird" template page in this book, to decorate your classroom with student work.

Make a Fourth of July Noisemaker!

Your students will love making a Fourth of July noisemaker! Supplies include two pie tins for each student; dried beans; red, white, and blue crepe paper; a stapler; and a glue stick.

Student instructions:

1. Cut six equal strips of crepe paper. Lay one edge of the strips in the pie pan and glue securely. (The rest of the strips should hang down below the pie pan.)

2. Pour half a cup of dried beans in the pie tin.

3. Place another pie tin on top and staple all around the edges. Shake your noisemakers on the Fourth of July!

Goods and Services Collage

You will need old magazines, two pieces of poster board, and glue. Ask students to cut out pictures showing goods and services from magazines. Have them sort the pictures into two stacks—one for goods and one for services. Label each poster with a large headline—either GOODS or SERVICES. Then, help your students make two class collages to demonstrate their understanding of the two concepts.

VOCABULARY (side 1)

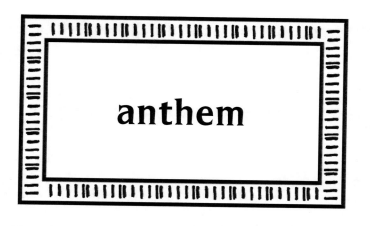

anthem

community

authority figure

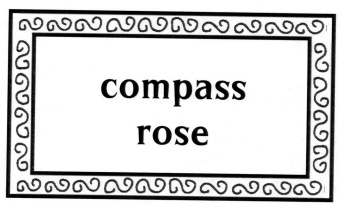

compass rose

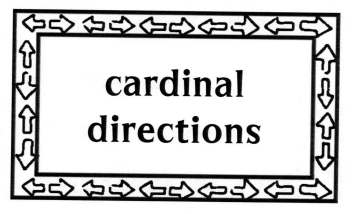

cardinal directions

consequence

celebrate

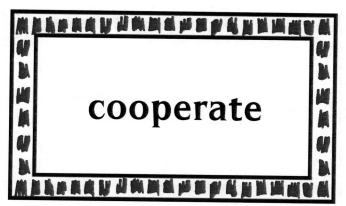

cooperate

VOCABULARY (side 2)

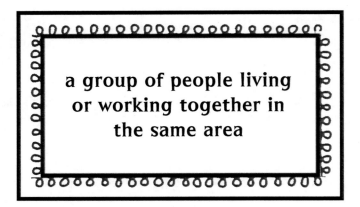
a group of people living or working together in the same area

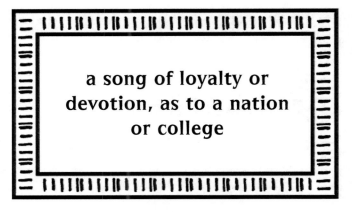
a song of loyalty or devotion, as to a nation or college

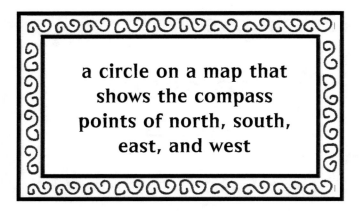
a circle on a map that shows the compass points of north, south, east, and west

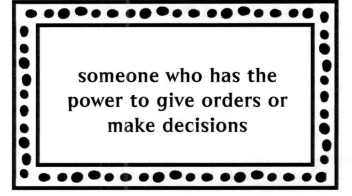
someone who has the power to give orders or make decisions

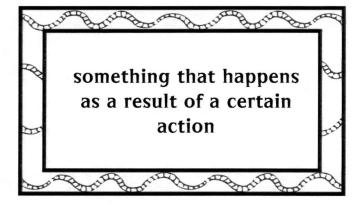
something that happens as a result of a certain action

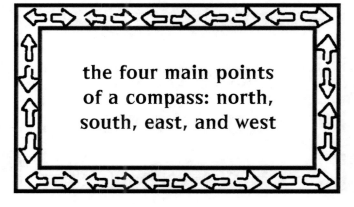
the four main points of a compass: north, south, east, and west

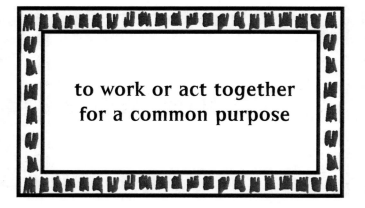
to work or act together for a common purpose

to do something special or enjoyable for a special event, occasion, or holiday

VOCABULARY (side 1)

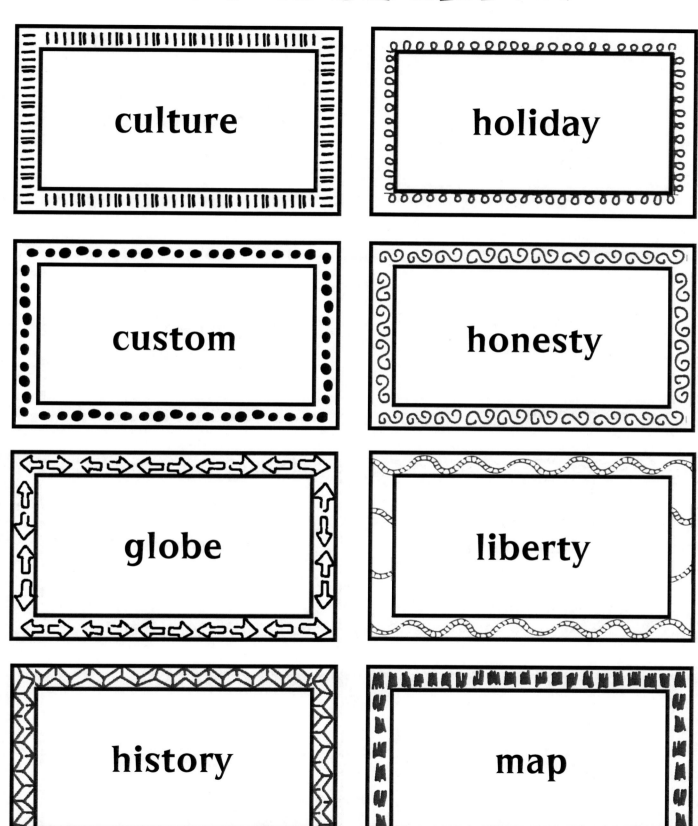

culture

holiday

custom

honesty

globe

liberty

history

map

VOCABULARY (side 2)

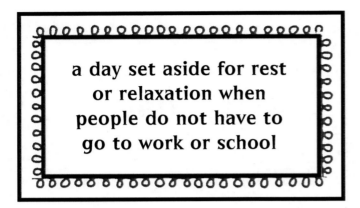
a day set aside for rest or relaxation when people do not have to go to work or school

the way of life and customs of a certain group of people

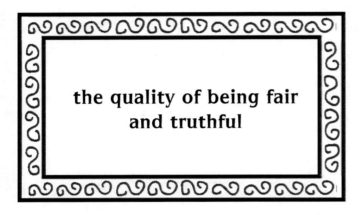
the quality of being fair and truthful

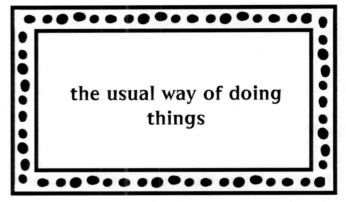
the usual way of doing things

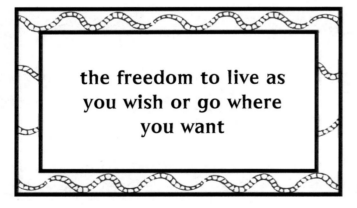
the freedom to live as you wish or go where you want

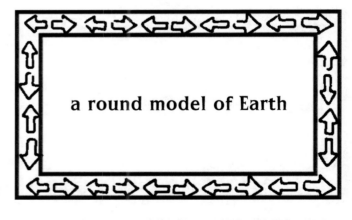
a round model of Earth

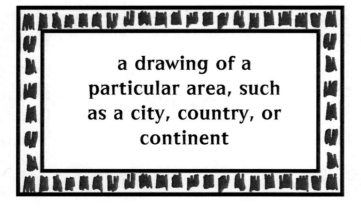
a drawing of a particular area, such as a city, country, or continent

events of the past

VOCABULARY (side 1)

map legend

self-control

patriotism

symbol

respect

tradition

responsible

veteran

VOCABULARY (side 2)

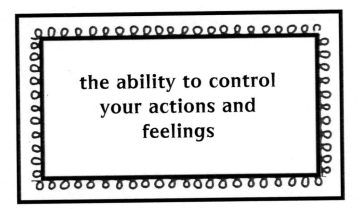

the ability to control your actions and feelings

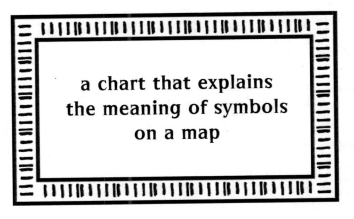

a chart that explains the meaning of symbols on a map

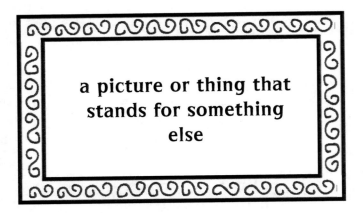

a picture or thing that stands for something else

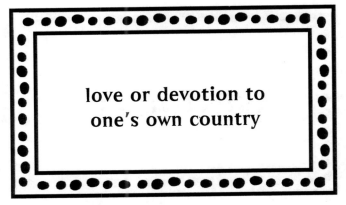

love or devotion to one's own country

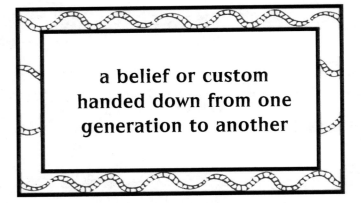

a belief or custom handed down from one generation to another

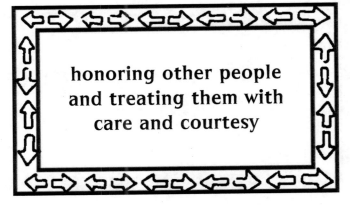

honoring other people and treating them with care and courtesy

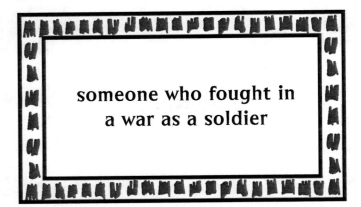

someone who fought in a war as a soldier

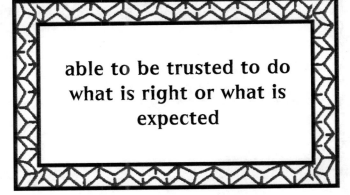

able to be trusted to do what is right or what is expected